Happy C

N/c

Rec. 1110.

WKLP

Ali Ross
Skiing Clinic

in association with Audi

Audi

Ali Ross
Skiing Clinic

in association with Audi

Cross Publishing
Chale, Isle of Wight

First Published in Great Britain in 1998 by Cross Publishing,
Chale, Isle of Wight.

A CIP catalogue record for this book is available from the
British Library.

ISBN 1 873295 36 7

Design by Anita Govinden, Digital Artwork by PM Colour Ltd.
Isle of Wight.
Printed and Bound by Butler and Tanner,
Frome, Somerset.

contents

acknowledgements

Special thanks to Audi UK, who made this book possible and who have long supported the sport of skiing and Ali Ross Skiing Clinics. Thanks are also due for the supply to the Skiing Clinics of the Audi quattro car, ensuring we could get to the ski resorts when others could not.

Additional thanks are due to the following companies and organisations:

Salomon (Freedom Action Sports Specialists), who provided our skis, boots and bindings and to whom we would like to offer our thanks for their support of the Skiing Clinics since their inception.

The ski clothing manufacturers Omega UK and Spyder, France provided Ali Ross with the ski suits worn by him for this book.

Revo sunglasses, from Bausch and Lomb.

The Ski Club of Great Britain for giving us access to their archive photographs of racers.

The following individuals contributions should also be mentioned:

Moira Ross, without whose skill with words, ability to take the photographs and intimate knowledge of the Skiing Clinics system, this project would still have been in the making.

Guy Clarey, Ski Fast sports shop in Tignes, former ESF director.

Jean Louis Ottobon, ESF director, Tignes, France. Both Guy and Jean Louis have given me invaluable help - and advice - over my many years in Tignes, for which I would like to express my profound thanks.

Bill O'Connell, Vail Associates and Robin Brown, Breckenridge Ski School, USA for their help during our trips to their resorts.

And finally, to all my pupils - without whom this ski teaching business would not exist...

ALASDAIR ROSS

introduction

Skiers arrive in the mountains with all kinds of motives in mind. You may simply want to relax and enjoy your holiday skiing leisurely around the pistes or you may dream about venturing into the wilder places far away from busy resorts. All skiers, though have one thing in common - they want to improve. And unfortunately, a second thing they have in common is that improvement is too often elusive. You feel you can achieve more, but don't know how to. It can happen at any stage. Intermediate and advanced skiers suffer from it and it may be some consolation to know that racers are afflicted as well. It is a frustrating experience. For the average holiday skier, the world of the expert seems like a far-away mountain top on a bad day - remote, unattainable and shrouded in clouds. There are other factors which stand in the way of improvement.

Fear can be one reason that people feel limited in their skiing. By its nature, it is not always susceptible to logical solutions. What people often forget is that fear is sometimes a sensible warning device. We are sometimes right to be afraid. So never feel "chicken" if you turn back at the top of a difficult run and descend by a less demanding path. There is no point in terrifying yourself and doing a lot of mental, if not physical harm, by attempting runs which are really beyond you, egged on by "friends". I have seen a lot of skiers who aren't that skilful technically, who get down by sheer bravado. They may well enjoy their skiing for a long time, but courage in the long run usually fails and then what do you do? I've also taught people who by their nature are quite timid, who once they prove to themselves how the skis work and who have developed good natural technique, are eventually prepared to take on the worst of the Alps' black runs. This enables them to ski when fear alone might have been a deterrent. Nothing succeeds in overcoming these limitations better than a good understanding of techniques. We can learn then, not to be afraid: but don't try to eliminate what I call the "helpful" type of fear - natural caution has kept me alive in the mountains. Be aware that one day it may save you.

Another consideration for the two-week-a-year skier is that the movements used in skiing, though perfectly natural, often feel strange because you're not in the habit of using them. Living as many people do in urban environments, this is not surprising. You stand upright, you probably often sit in offices and so when you ski, you have to think again about developing awareness of what is being asked of you. As you will see, we have to bend and modify the body's posture to cope with travelling at speed over rough terrain. We no longer feel "normal". We have to test our mental awareness in an unfamiliar and sometimes hostile environment. To have all of this said to you whilst you are no doubt sitting comfortably reading this book, is one thing. To be aware of how it translates into skiing is another.

The dream of most skiers is to be able to ski anywhere, effectively. But often, we are in a hurry to be seen to improve. We want to look like good skiers first. "Looking good" is often an aim in itself. One might well ask, *"What is style?".* The impression of good skiing creates misinterpretations of the picture we see. For instance, an effective skier's performance might produce the words "elegant", "graceful", and "effortless". All of these impressions are the effect of good techniques. By posing one's arms, legs and shoulders in a taught stance, one can arrive at a quite reasonable simulation of good skiing, without skiing well at all.

What is it that creates good skiing?

As my own ideas about ski technique and how people learn have evolved over the years, so a better understanding of the source of the problems and a possible solution began to emerge. Most of the problems come from misunderstandings and misinterpretations of basic technical concepts at the very beginning. Unless we have a crystal clear idea of the fundamentals - the three ingredients which have never and will never change; how the ski works - how the body works, and thirdly how the forces generated in a turn affect us - we will always sooner or later find that progress slows down, apparently inexplicably.

I believe that anyone can ski better than they ever thought possible, given the willingness to experiment with a few basic ideas. The Skiing Clinics came into being in response to what I saw as the need for an independent system of teaching these ingredients of effective technique - the fundamental concepts which produce excellence in skiing. To get the most out of your precious time on skis, to be able to achieve your goals in skiing, you should first understand what *creates* good skiing. My aim in this book is to help you do just that.

Karl Schranz, 1958.

Thomas Stangassinger, 1998.
Other than equipment, in forty years, little has changed.

1. the learning curve

"To improve is to change, but to be perfect is to have changed many times".

(The late John Pipe, one of my favourite pupils).

Progress in skiing, I believe, comes not through following step-by-step set pieces but rather through a thorough understanding and awareness of what is responsible for creating good skiing. If you look at the development of Alpine skiing, no one suddenly "invented" a snow-plough turn and then a parallel turn. Parallel skiing evolved as the natural outcome of people just skiing faster once they'd gained some confidence. These developments were, however, soon labelled and analysed into parts and taught as sequential steps. "First you do A, then B, followed by C...". You may get the first, second and even third steps right, but then typically it all falls apart. Trying harder only compounds the problem. It is unsurprising given this approach, that most holiday skiers have only the vaguest of ideas about what is actually happening when they ski down a mountain side.

How do we overcome these problems? Skiing lessons involve a lot of listening, seeing and doing. Sports psychologists quote the following observations: we forget 90 per cent of what we hear, but we remember 50 per cent of what we see and hear, and 90 per cent of what we do. However, simply "seeing" may not be very useful as an aid to our own performance if we don't understand what *creates* the picture. For instance, if you watch a world-class slalom racer, you see a picture of flowing movements, which is often described as

"graceful" or "effortless"; but this by itself doesn't help us to learn what creates the images we observe. Such visual aid can be actually detrimental if we misinterpret it. Similarly, "doing" by itself is rarely helpful if we misunderstand what it is we are supposed to be doing. So, before "seeing" and "doing" can become relevant to our learning, we must retrace our steps and return to basic technical concepts if we want to overcome the limitations imposed by these misunderstandings and misinterpretations.

To do this, you may find that you are presented with a challenging prospect. You are no longer a beginner, you may indeed be quite experienced and adept on skis, but to have come as far as you have along the learning path and then to be asked to go back and re-examine basics is not always easy. There is much "unlearning" to be done. In practice, this means that you must be ready to accept change, and that often makes people feel uncomfortable. Physically too, change can present a challenge, especially when you've built up skiing habits over the years. You do, after all, already know another way of skiing.

What you have always done in the past may stubbornly stay with you without you even being aware of it. Pupils are sometimes surprised to the point of disbelief if I tell them that their old habits are still there. This, incidentally, is the reason I think video is so vital as a learning aid. Although they call it the "horror movie", once Skiing Clinics first-time clients have got over the initial "Oh, God, that's me!" reaction, they can begin to use it constructively. So to start with, developing effective skiing positions and movements will feel different, even very different from what you're used to. With practice, however, the exercises will soon become familiar, even second nature, I hope.

Nothing changes from the most basic to the most advanced levels of skiing, if you learn effective techniques from the beginning. As you progress, the approach is modified slightly, but the essentials remain the same, regardless of conditions. Once you have understood what creates good skiing and have experienced the ideas working in practice, what you do thereafter will take you almost anywhere you want to go in the mountains.

This book, like the Skiing Clinics themselves, should be regarded as a training programme. It is one means of overcoming the limitations which one way or another prevent improvement in skiing performance. Its natural readership will be found amongst skiers who want to improve and who are willing to change.

Practising the exercises soon becomes familiar.

2. concepts

In many ways, it is not surprising that recreational skiers have a less than clear idea of basic concepts. By the time they have skied a few seasons, they will probably have had lessons in many different countries, each with a distinctive national ski school approach and with little over-arching agreement between them. What you are taught will vary, perhaps considerably. So, a holiday skier taught to ski in say, Switzerland, will have received different information from someone taught in France, and so on.

Yet if you watch the top ten slalom or giant slalom skiers in the World Cup, who hail from all of the top Alpine skiing nations and beyond, what is the most striking feature of their performances? When I put this question to Skiing Clinics pupils, the answer is always unequivocal. "They all look identical".

The explanation is simple. The top racers, regardless of nationality, use the same basic technique, based on fundamental concepts. So they are all actually skiing technically in the same way. In the split second it takes to win or lose a race, there is no room for confusion about how they change direction. Before you say, "what has this got to do with me?", it is important not to dismiss the comparison with racers. The stress felt by the best slalom skiers in the World Cup is similar to what you might feel negotiating a particularly difficult red run. Therefore, if you don't have the same clear idea of skiing technique, you can't expect to perform well at any level. To be able to turn effectively, where and when you want is the key to better performance. And to understand this, we must first examine the most important factor in skiing-the ski itself.

The *ski* will turn *you*

This is not self-evident to most skiers and may well be contrary to what the vast majority believe happens as they ski down the mountain. You have probably been taught that you turn the skis - according to national preferences, the way of doing so varies, as we have said - but the message remains the same. Yet fundamental to any understanding of ski technique is this single point, which once explained and then worked upon in practice can utterly transform the progress of the holiday skier. The point could hardly sound more simple and it is by no means a new discovery, but I never cease to be amazed that most people spend their entire skiing lives never having heard it.

From the time that Alpine skis were first used, the ski has been designed as a turning machine. It will turn you - if you know how to use it. Over the years, skis have become very sophisticated turning machines indeed, with huge amounts of skill, time and money invested in developing them further. Modern skis, of course, with the latest technological inputs, look very different from their ancestral counterparts, but the essential characteristics of the ski have not changed.

If you pick up your skis and look along their length, what you see is a graceful curve - the ski's "side-cut". Wide at the heel and tip, narrower in the approximate middle. This curve will vary according to the type of ski, but its function is essentially the same in all skis. Side-cut is the key to the modern ski's turning abilities.

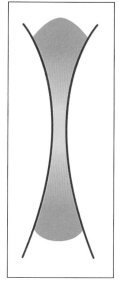

Other important factors also influence this, but for the time being let's concentrate on how you can make the ski's turning characteristic work for you.

On the move, when the ski is put on its edge and pressure is applied, it will bend in an arc and carry you round with it, as if you are on rails.

The forces in the turn

The concept that the ski will turn us, if it is on its edge and bent in an arc, is very different from the commonly accepted idea that we physically turn the ski. There is also a second aspect to this concept which is important - once we accept that the ski will turn us, then the body gets much more positive feedback and is able to react to the forces set up in the turn in a very natural way. Any heavy object travelling at speed in a curve is subjected to several forces. The one that we are most concerned with, and that you as a skier become most aware of, is the force that pulls you to the outside of the turn. To ski effectively, you must be able to resist this force, because otherwise it would be impossible to keep the skis on their edges throughout the turn. The body already knows how to do this, with little or no instruction, provided it can sense what is happening.

There are some other sports in which people make movements that are identical to those of a good skier, *without being taught how to*. Roller-skaters and in-line skaters are two examples. The secret is that they get positive feedback through friction between the wheels of the skate and the road and this gives the body the information it needs to react to the forces involved, with an entirely natural movement. No one needs to teach them this. What is also interesting is that if it rains, producing a slippery surface, many of them say that they don't even try to skate - after all, who wants to fall on concrete?

Notice the movements and compare them to those of a good skier. I call this natural angulation. Indeed, several top ski racers train in the summer on Alpine roads using such skates.

Skidding and Carving

So if the body can respond naturally to the forces generated in the turn, why do we need to be taught? I believe that the answer is quite simple. In the very nature of skiing, we are standing on a sliding base and on a slippery surface (Remember the skaters who wouldn't train on a wet day?) Since there is much less friction, the body receives confusing information. It doesn't like the feeling of what I call "stereo motion" - moving forwards and sideways simultaneously, especially at speed downhill. Everyone recognises the feeling of insecurity if you happen to step unexpectedly on a patch of ice in the street. In skiing, if our concept of turning is to push the skis around the turn, skidding the skis, then we only tend to increase this existing feeling of insecurity. Indeed, this way of turning contains the very ingredients which land us on the "plateau". It limits us to being able to ski well only in the ideal conditions of a perfect piste, blue skies and sunshine. Should any aspect of these ideal conditions not prevail, the performance of most recreational skiers will probably deteriorate quite drastically. Take away blue skies and perfect pistes and in their place put poor visibility, ice, deep snow or bumps and many skiers have problems.

Let me explain why. In perfect conditions, even if we turn by forcing the skis into a physically-induced skid, the skis will work for us by default. They sink slightly into the packed snow, and don't skid too much so the body gets some positive feedback, enabling us to cope - we feel happier and less unstable. On ice, however, this idea of turning produces excessive skidding, which makes us feel afraid and generally out of control. In deep snow, there is resistance to the skis skidding sideways, and so trying to turn by skidding flat skis doesn't work at all. On the other hand, if our concept of turning is to use the skis to turn us, travelling in curves along the edges - the feeling is like being carried around on rails - this creates much more positive feedback in all conditions. The body then can respond by angulating naturally and thereby resisting the force generated in the turn. This technique, often called "carving the turn" is almost always regarded by experts as one for advanced skiers only - even just for racers, according to some opinions.

I believe that holiday skiers are not only able to use this concept of turning at their own speeds and level of skill, but also that unless this basic principle is learned, they will be limited in their skiing progress. The degree of "carving" or "skidding" in a turn should depend on one thing - the level of skill of the skier and not a totally different concept of turning.

3. experiments

Basic stance on skis

The first morning of the course and one of the first questions to sort out is how we stand on our skis. Problems of skiing posture can often be self-correcting. By this I mean that once you have understood and experienced how the skis will work for you, a good basic stance tends to develop with no further instruction. However, there is something of "a chicken and an egg" here, because whilst poor posture is often the result of misunderstood skiing technique, so also can one's technical progress be inhibited by misconceptions about stance or posture on skis.

What then is a good skiing stance? We walk around every day of our lives in a fairly normal, upright way. You've also probably had it drummed into you as a child to stand up straight and not to slouch. However, good posture for skiing is different. Our normal stance has to be modified quite a bit to produce a good skiing stance. This is because the demands of moving on skis over changing terrain, perhaps at a fair speed, mean that we have to flex and bend much more than we're used to. The body positions and movements which we need to adopt to produce effective skiing responses involve flexing the ankles, knees and torso. The legs turn into shock absorbers or springs, ready to adjust to different conditions. But often in relation to how they stand on their skis, my pupils tell me that the first instruction they ever received as beginners was "don't stick your bottom out!" or " stand up!" This was no doubt intended to correct the typical example of ineffective posture which you can spot in the beginners' classes - and beyond. Skiers often react to these exhortations by standing bolt upright instead, so that your bottom is no longer stuck out, but I'm afraid that you are still not in a good skiing stance. Many pupils who come to my clinics for the first time stand on their skis in a far too upright way as a result of this misinterpretation.

To correct this, what you should do is to rock forward at the *ankles as well as the knees* with the shin pressing forward, feeling the front of the boot quite firmly. The body is still flexed at the waist to a certain degree. The effect is an "S" shape. Remember the feet are about hip-width apart.

No bend at all in the ankles and knees and excessive bending forward from the waist, combine to produce the definitely inelegant, stuck-out derriere.

When I ask my pupils to do this for the first time, everyone is surprised by how much they need to bend and flex in the right places to produce this good overall stance. It doesn't feel "normal" to them. They say they feel almost "hunched up" or "inelegant". However, this doesn't mean that it's wrong.

Here is an exercise that I have used for many years to increase awareness of posture. You can experiment with it almost anywhere. Try it standing on the flat first, stationary, then find a gentle slope and try it on the move. Just try straight running downhill. Experiment by stretching up as high as you can and then crouching down low. Get the feel of the range of movement possible. If you grade your most upright position as 10 and your lowest as 1, then a reasonable position for skiing would be between 5 and 7. It will vary depending on your own physical conformation.

When you bend at the waist, beware! It should not produce a hollow lower back. Hollowness here inhibits the movements you need to be able to make to ski well. Remember - think of the "S" shape. To me, having spent years on skis, this stance has become second nature. If you visualise the image of good posture every time before you set off downhill, until you do it automatically, you may be surprised how much your general skiing will improve. Good posture in skiing, though, is only the beginning. When we're moving, our positions and movements in skiing, I believe, are entirely natural reactions to the dynamics of skiing, and not actions which can be taught. Given the right conditions of feedback, the body will adopt quite natural positions without being given specific set instructions about what to do.

Turning - feel how the ski works

Understanding the basic concepts which I have been describing is one thing. Doing it is another.

Firstly, we have to experiment with a few training exercises which are designed to help you feel how the ski works. Because you already know how to ski a different way, you have developed skiing habits which by their nature, will produce automatic reactions the minute you set off down the slope. So, in this first experiment, I am going to ask you to "short-circuit" these ingrained responses.

Find a gentle, wide slope, preferably one that you know and that has a run out at the bottom, so that you can concentrate on the exercise alone. Stand with skis about hip width apart, in an open parallel, facing downhill and let the skis begin the slide down the fall-line, gathering some speed. Put one hand firmly on the side of the thigh, about half way down, and then really press the leg progressively inwards. Notice in the picture how the legs and the hip lie inwards towards the centre of the turn. You should feel that you are being carried around in a curve. Try it again pushing the other leg. One side may well feel better than the other - we're all one-sided to some extent, tending to favour the "stronger" side. Practice this exercise for as long as necessary to give you the feeling of the skis turning you.

At this early stage, I emphasise trying half turns first, from the fall-line to the traverse. Most skiers have regarded the fall-line - the line of least resistance down the slope - as the "panic zone" at one time or another. We want to get through it as quickly as possible, which tends to make us force the skis around - exactly what we want to avoid. To develop a feeling of what the ski can do for you, we need to eliminate as many distractions as possible. This is also the reason for choosing a non-threatening slope to start with, which has a relatively shallow fall-line.

Why do you have to physically push the leg in order to feel the ski working? After all, we don't ski about

First experiment - getting the ski on its edge.

Edge **before** the fall-line...

then progressive degrees of edge.

the mountain like that. In experimenting with new ways of doing things, the very unfamiliarity itself makes us feel strange. We have been taught a whole range of actions - up and down movements, unweighting, shifting weight and so on - which hitherto, has formed the basis of our current skiing habits. I teach this exercise *because* it helps to "short circuit" the skiing habits which have accumulated over the years. The exercise is vital and is the key to all future progress.

The next stage is to try the same exercise through a complete turn. It is important to emphasise *progressive* pushing of the leg, since the skis are on their edges more and more as the turn is completed. Start on whichever side you feel most comfortable with. The turning ski (the uphill ski at this stage) should *already be on its edge on the traverse* if the turn is to be effective. In other words, the ski should already be on its edge well *before* the fall-line. The ski bends, its side-cut begins to work for you and you are deflected towards the fall-line. The ski also accelerates. This is the point at which many skiers have felt a pang of fear, not wanting to shoot out of control downhill. But as long as the ski is on its edge, it will continue to curve into *and out of* the fall-line, back onto the traverse, in control. The fall-line then is no longer a line down which to run out of control, but merely a dot on the curve described by the turning ski.

The deliberate pushing of the leg increases the degree to which the ski is on its edge as it turns. In the Skiing Clinics, I ask pupils to visualise the different amount of edge in this way; if you are standing on the slope just above me as I start a turn, you should be able to see some of the sole of my ski; if you are standing opposite as I travel into the fall-line, you should see half of the sole and if you stand below me at the finish of the turn, you should be able to see almost the whole sole of the ski.

The finish of the turn is, of course, important too. Having progressively put the ski on its edge, we must make sure we finish the turn with the skis firmly on their edges. It may help to "count" your way through the turn - one two three four five six, like half of the face of a clock, with six representing maximum edge.

The ski is 45° on its edge.

The end of the turn - the whole sole of the ski.

At this stage, don't do too many turns. I always say to the Skiing Clinic pupils that I would rather see two or three good turns than half a dozen mediocre ones!

It would, however, be surprising if some of the old habits hadn't crept up on you, even in this basic exercise. Almost all of the problems are caused by old habits, principally the urge to turn the ski. Take the word "turning" itself. It has strong rotational implications. You interpret this to mean that you turn the ski. You may understand the concept that skis on their edges will turn you, but previously trained habits die hard. Despite yourself, you may still try to force turn the ski to turn, especially through the fall line. It is important to concentrate on simply putting the ski on its edge to start the turn and then *allow the ski to travel into the fall-line*. Remember control comes from the degree of edge applied, not from heaving the skis around. You should practise, practise, practise this exercise until it becomes second nature - in much the same way you trained your old habits, so the new ones have to be trained. My pupils have time in the course to go off on their own and do just that. We also use video on day one so that they can see their interpretations of information received to date and also because, without an awareness of what you are doing now, how can you change it?

"Reaching out" to help angulation.

The foundations of good skiing therefore, are made with this basic technique. Trainers of Olympic ski teams have their racers practise exactly the same exercise on equally undemanding terrain, so you are in good company in this respect and are not the only ones, therefore running about the mountain pushing the leg in with the hand. Once you have really grasped the point of the exercise and more importantly, felt the ski working for you, you will be able to put the ski on its edge *without* physically pressing the leg with the hand. At this stage, the feeling should be one of projecting the knees and hips across the skis, towards the fall-line. Sounds committing to do, but remember you are moving and the forces in the turn will prevent you from falling over.

Angulation

We saw in the last chapter that it is important to be able to resist effectively the centrifugal force which will pull you over the outside of the turn - the opposite of what we want to achieve. So the next stage is to develop angulation, which in turn makes it easier to put the ski on its edge. We try this next exercise stationary first of all. Stand on the traverse, again with the feet about hip-width apart and reach as far downhill as possible with the arm, the ski pole touching the downhill slope, leaning the hips and leg inwards. It may help to get another member of the group to stand downhill and try to pull you over sideways by taking hold of your arm and pulling to simulate the forces in the turn. To stop yourself from being pulled over, your natural reaction is to resist the force by leaning the hips and legs away from the source of the pull - and the result is natural angulation. Instead of standing still on the flat and having someone pull you over, we're now going to introduce the real thing - moving downhill, on a fairly wide, gentle slope. I say this because it is testing enough to try to unlearn old habits and to experiment with new ideas without being inhibited by the terrain. Move off from a fairly shallow traverse to start with, with feet apart, and as you feel yourself picking up some speed, reach out as far as you can with your arm to the outside of the turn, stretching as if to touch the slope and draw an arc in the snow.

As is the case with edge exercises, reaching out must be progressively greater throughout the turn. When I ski I do feel that I'm reaching out as much as this, so if it feels odd for the first few attempts, don't mistake this feeling of strangeness for doing something wrong. It is important to realise that the point of this exercise is not what the arm may be doing, but the angulated position thereby created - legs and hips, which are the centre of mass of the body, leaning to the centre of the turn and therefore off-setting the force which is pulling you to the outside of the turn.

4. the parallel turn

The pursuit of the perfect parallel turn is something of a Holy Grail to most skiers at some point. More advanced ski school classes are graded according to how well you can "ski parallel" and with the snow plough and stem classes left behind, what I call "parallelitis" begins to afflict you. The defining symptom is that you want to pull the skis together in an attempt to create the appearance of stylish skiing. There is so much emphasis on it that it's no surprise that you try to copy what you see - the appearance of legs and feet coming closer together. But mistaking the effect - the skis and legs coming closer - for the cause, will only produce what I called earlier the simulation of effective skiing, not the real thing. You cannot learn to ski parallel correctly simply by physically bringing the skis closer together.

So what is responsible for creating a good parallel turn?

The explanation is to be found in the effect of forces again. As you speed up, the force pulling you to the outside of the turn is greater. This creates more pressure on the turning ski and less on the inside ski, which will drift inwards towards the turning ski. The *effect* - the legs coming closer together - is purely the *result* of what is happening as we ski faster. The usual misinterpretation arises because we think this effect is produced by the physical action on our part of bringing the skis together. Just remember as you go faster, greater reaction from you is needed to resist the force pulling you over. You have to react with greater

movement - inwards with the legs and hips to the centre of the turn, away from the pull - as the force increases. You will find that as you go faster you will be skiing parallel naturally without thinking about the relation of one ski to the other.

There is only one difference between the snow-plough turn and the parallel turn - speed. You cannot perform a technically correct parallel turn without some speed. I am aware that to some, this is rather a heretical statement. The parallel turn needs de-bunking, since there is no great mystery involved in its execution, once you have understood the basic principles which underpin skiing. You may have noticed when you've been practising edge and angulation exercises, that you began to ski faster without trying to and as you did so, the skis started to come closer together. This is no accident; you were skiing parallel as the *result* of harnessing the main ingredients of effective skiing - how the skis work, the forces in the turn and how our bodies respond naturally to those forces, without consciously bringing your skis together and without anyone telling you "now you must ski parallel".

I have said before that at the start of the turn, I feel that I have to commit myself by projecting my knees and hips towards the fall line, putting the ski on its edge and angulating - otherwise how would I turn effectively? But unless you're used to trusting that the skis will take you through that "panic zone" as you reach the fall line, then I realise that you will not find it easy, until you prove it for yourself on a regular basis.

With some pressure on the upper edge of the top ski,
project the knees and hips downhill.

Here is an exercise that besides testing your degree of commitment, will help your parallel turns enormously. It is quite advanced and you can't do it slowly. Start in a steep traverse across a wide run so that you gather speed. Then begin to run along the top (upper) edge of the upper ski, by putting more pressure there. Now for the commitment. Whilst you hold the pressure on the upper edge of the top ski, project the knees and hips downhill.

You should feel an instant response. The ski whips you around very quickly. There is less resultant pressure on the other ski and so both skis naturally come closer together. A simple edge change is all that is needed and adjusting your stance so that there is more pressure on what is the uphill ski at this stage of the turn, in addition avoids the temptation to force the ski around in an erratic skid.

The ski poles

We often reach almost the end of a course and someone observes that I have hardly mentioned the pieces of equipment which often cause so much difficulty about how and when they should be wielded.

The reason is that poles, used in the way in which you have usually been taught, produce the "now you've got to turn" response, so the "computer programme" runs, you stab the snow, hang on and hope that a turn will happen as a result. I call this the "lamppost" effect and it is not at all helpful.

On the other hand, I think is equally unhelpful to ask experienced skiers at this stage in the learning curve, to do without poles altogether. If you've tried skiing without poles, you can begin to see why they're useful. You feel odd without them, you feel less balanced and as people have often said, you feel like a cat without whiskers.

I also find that once pupils have begun to feel the ski working for them, after a period of time planting the pole drops into the turn quite naturally. Commitment, as you know, is especially important at the beginning of the turn. The most committing movement is when we change edge to start our next turn. This is where the pole can be helpful. At the crucial point of changing edge, the pole will give you support. This timing is more important than exact directions about where you put the pole. There are some points that you should be aware of though. The planting of the pole shouldn't get in the way of our forward momentum, so you shouldn't plant it too close to the body or the skis. It also most often causes problems if we haven't anticipated the impact of the pole hitting the snow. If we don't *stiffen* the arm to take account of this impact, the body will be rotated and the shoulder thrown back. Just remember that at the time you plant the pole, this action should not affect the body's position. Allow the body's forward momentum to take the pole out of the snow.

As you change edge, the pole gives support.

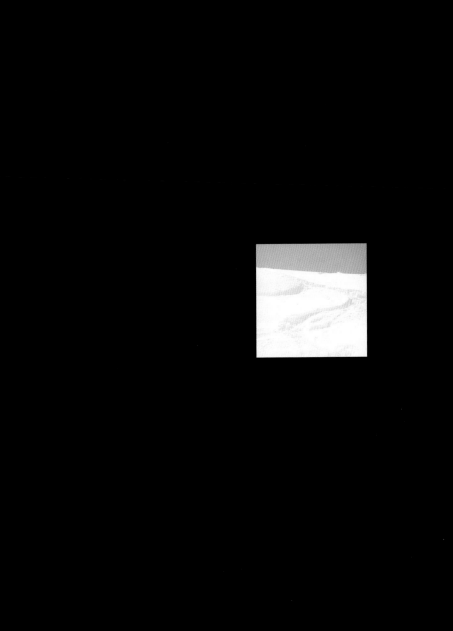

5. interpretations

There are commands in conventional instruction which every intermediate and advanced skier will have heard. Unfortunately, these instructions are easily misinterpreted and this is frequently directly responsible for much confusion and failure to make progress. Most of the questions I am asked by skiers who are first-timers on a Skiing Clinic relate to what they have been taught previously about what constitutes ski technique. Let us take the more common ones.

"Skiers make up and down movements"

Undoubtedly in your skiing past, you will have been told that skiers make "up and down" movements.

You probably think of this as you might do in normal, everyday life - if someone tells you to "go up and then go down", I'd guess that you might stand up straight and then bend as if you were going to sit. You've followed the instruction perfectly. And if that was how I thought "up and down" movements happened in skiing, then I wouldn't be able to ski either. It is true that when we watch a good skier, we see increases and decreases of height. But what *creates* this effect? Not the straightening and bending described above, but something else. The result - the ups and downs - is produced by the body's natural responses to the forces generated in the turn.

We angulate during the turn, reducing height.

At the beginning of the next turn, we return to a neutral position, thereby increasing height. This gives the impression of the skier making "up and down" movements. Remember that the effect - ups and downs - is produced by the body's natural responses to the forces generated in the turn.

"You must shift your weight onto the turning ski"

This is probably the most used and misunderstood instruction of all. It is easy to see why. You walk down the street every day in life, shifting your weight from one foot to the other without thinking about it. And so, is it surprising that when it comes to skiing, you do what comes automatically? As an illustration, I ask my pupils to "shift their weight" and everyone follows my instruction to the letter. They stand on one foot. In skiing too, they interpret this command to transfer weight as they would if they were walking along the road, shifting their weight from one foot to the other.

It *is* true that when you ski, pressure distribution changes. In America, they have demonstrated this by putting pressure-sensitive pads under the skis and wiring them up to show that there are increases and decreases of pressure throughout the turn. But what I would like you to think about is who or what is responsible for this pressure distribution? And secondly, how useful is it as a skier to be told to actively "shift your weight"?

The problem arises because if you shift your weight on to the turning ski, all this does is to flatten the ski and make it next to impossible to resist the outward pull in the turn. "Weight shift" is a *reaction to the forces in the turn* and not a deliberate action.

"The parallel turn is initiated by unweighting"

This brings us to yet another widely misunderstood phenomenon in skiing - "unweighting". It is conventionally accepted and taught that a parallel turn is initiated by unweighting the skis. So much emphasis is placed upon this phase of the turn that it is even described as the "magic ingredient" of all advanced manoeuvres. My view is that if, up to now,

we have required the ski to be on its edge, with pressure applied to it before we can turn effectively, then it does not appear to make a great deal of sense to argue that weight should be actively taken off the ski in order to initiate a turn. As we have already seen, parallel skiing evolves naturally, as a result of greater speed and movement, using exactly the same concept that we introduced at the very beginning. What is important is edge changing in initiating turns.

Here is a little food for thought. If you are travelling in a traverse at 10-15 m.p.h. and you "unweight" your skis, what happens? When I put this question to my pupils, the response is frequently less than certain. If you simply "unweight" your skis, you will carry on in the same direction - traversing! Inertia has the effect of keeping you going in the same direction all things being equal. You will only change direction when you change edge.

"Good skiers ski with their feet and legs together"

That good skiers ski "with their feet and legs together" is a notion that is less widely accepted nowadays than it was in the past. Modern skiing has moved on to the idea that to ski with your legs and feet glued together is not actually a very effective way of getting down the mountain. But it is still a prevalent misconception amongst many holiday skiers, and it is often seen as a "stylish" way to ski. As I explained earlier, this one impression alone has been responsible for more anguish and failure to improve than almost any other. Closing the feet together simply produces a simulation of effective skiing.

It is true that good skiers appear to ski with their legs relatively close together, but remember what is it that creates this appearance - the effects of speed and of angulation. The angulation of a good skier - leg lean, i.e. legs and hips to the centre of the turn. It is my contention that by leaving the feet at hip-width apart in skiing, we can achieve more effective leg lean, because the hips remain at more or less the same height, permitting easy and natural angulation. If the feet are held close together, when we try to lean the legs inwards with the feet in this position, one hip drops lower than the other, making angulation much more difficult. What does this mean in skiing terms? When you can resist the force, this means an effective body position, with the ski being held well on its edge, curving throughout the turn. It produces a feeling of great stability, a bit like being carried around on rails. If the feet are held deliberately close together, it is almost impossible to achieve sufficient leg lean to keep the skis on their edges, leading to excessive skidding.

"Good skiing looks effortless"

I agree that good skiing does look effortless. There can be few more beautiful sights in sport than a good skier in full flight through deep powder snow, a bump field or simply making flowing turns down a wide open run. The truly skilful performance has tremendous aesthetic appeal, so it is understandable why you should want to copy it. But how do you copy "gracefulness", "elegance", "effortlessness"? These words describe a picture, but as I have suggested already, such visual aids are of little use to us if we just try to imitate what we see, without knowing first what creates what we see. The impression of "effortlessness" is actually quite an accurate description of good skiing because technically efficient skiers use a minimum of physical input. Less skilful skiers use physical strength to force their skis to turn. The good skiers know that the ski is designed as a turning machine;

The legs appear to be together. This is a natural reaction to speed and the forces set up in a turn. It is not created by the physical action of bringing the skis together. The appearance is caused by the legs and hips having moved towards the centre of the turn to resist the outward pull.

The only effort required is to hold the skis on their edges.

when it is placed on its edge and pressure applied, it describes an arc, which carries the skier around. What creates the image of effortlessness is the positive feedback from the edged ski that allows the skier to feel the forces set up and then react to them with perfectly natural movements.

"Turn your shoulders to look down the valley".

If our shoulders are facing up the hill, this is caused by hip rotation. Pulling the shoulders round therefore to face down the valley will not correct the cause of the problem. It is true that a good skier does have the shoulders angled towards the valley at the end of a turn, and this is because the hip position is correct, inside the ski leaning to the centre of the turn. Again, it is a case of understanding the difference between cause and effect.

6. refining the turn

So far we have been concentrating on long radius turns. However, we need to be able to tighten our turns according to terrain - steeper slopes, bumps, narrow paths and so on. How much we put the ski on its edge and how quickly we can do this will produce different responses from the ski.

At this stage, you should experiment with different amounts of edge and how quickly you need to get the ski on its edge to produce a given radius of turn. This means practising more rapid inward leg movements. One of the main reasons holiday skiers find it hard to follow a pre-determined line - a field of bumps being the classic example - is because they can't change the radius adequately or quickly enough. I don't expect you to make an immediate transition between long turns and fall-line turns, so we practise tightening the radius gradually, again on a wide slope, where there is no pressure to *have* to turn. We gradually reduce the amount of time spent on the traverse, though it is important not to try to do too many shorter turns at this stage, since the tendency is to revert to forcing the skis around. Give yourself time to complete each medium radius turn before starting the next.

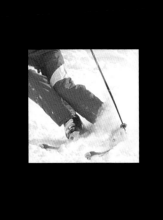

7. fall-line skiing

If parallel skiing has been a frustrating goal for many skiers, then linking parallel turns straight down the fall line has been another source of probably greater frustration. As we have found so often before, how you misinterpret what you see is responsible for many of these problems. Apparently the feet are being pushed from side to side. But if you try to copy this, you will at best only succeed in producing a simulation of fall-line skiing. And again, you find that you become limited to where and when you can do this. Every variation of fall-line skiing produces essentially the same illusion. You were in a chair-lift above a good skier making fall-line turns, you could see that the skis were following their length around the fall line and not, as it may appear, that they are being physically pushed by the skier from side to side.

The turning skis carry the feet to either side. Before I go any further, I would like you to consider something for a moment. As you move on to more advanced skiing, you aren't being asked to perform something which is completely different from what went before. Many skiers believe that snow-plough turns are an inferior species, different in kind from parallel turns, and that more advanced parallel turns are at yet another remove from both. But from the most basic to the most advanced forms of skiing nothing changes I believe. How we apply our technique is modified slightly, to take account of speed, terrain and faster reactions, but the essentials remain the same. Take a look at the parallel turns we've been practising so far and at the tighter variation which we call "fall-line" turns.

Trajectory of body

Trajectory of ski

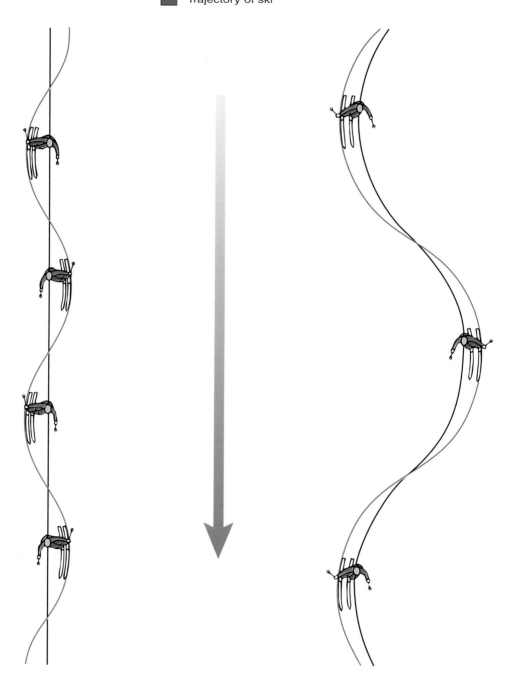

Long parallel turns mean turn, traverse, turn, traverse. Fall-line turns eliminate the traverse. We commit ourselves to the next turn at the moment we finish the last one. The difference is this. In our long parallel turns, the body is following the same direction as the skis. In fall-line turns, the body is moving in one direction - straight down the fall-line - whereas our skis are turning either side of that line, crossing the body's trajectory. What happens is that providing you stabilise the upper body, the turning effect of the skis causes energy to be progressively built up in the legs. "Stabilising" means keeping the hips and shoulders facing down the fall line and so resisting the turning effect which the skis have on the body.

The natural balancing aids - the arms - also help us in this. As the turn finishes, your body's direction of travel crosses that of the skis, the built-up energy is released and helps you to change edge by projecting the legs from the end of the last turn towards the fall line. A firm pole plant can be a very effective aid to this release of energy. It also helps to stabilise the upper body. To describe the dynamics in fall-line skiing, I use what I call the "rubber block" effect. The turning effect of the skis is strong and people are often surprised by how much they have to resist it by stabilising the upper body to face down the fall line.

The rebound effect.

It takes practice, but we have nothing that is really new to learn. Although movements need to be quick and precise to react to the stronger forces involved, they are not different from what you've already done. The initial inward movement of the knees and hips puts the ski on its edge and the follow-through progressively keeps it there. In fall-line skiing, ideally the energy build-up is released so that the edges change without any effort on your part. But as before, to become aware of the degree of movement needed, we return to basics. We want to get the feel of moving straight down the fall line, without traversing, so we choose a moderate slope, one on which you feel comfortable. Try our original exercise of pushing the leg in with the hand, this time making the knee movements sharper and stronger in order to tighten the radius of the turn. Remember to

coordinate the inward movement of knees with that of the hips. If the terrain which you've chosen is not too difficult, you should be able to make tighter turns than you've been used to.

I must stress that to get effective control in the fall line, we have to use stronger and sharper knee movements. Until you get used to the feeling and effects of skiing in the fall line, there are a few common difficulties which most skiers encounter. To start with. I sometimes find that it helps to remind ourselves of why we want to master fall-line skiing. There are times and places when long turns won't do. On steeper slopes or narrow tracks and gullies, for instance, fall-line turns are often all we can perform if we're to get down at all. So they're an essential part of skiing, enabling us to go virtually anywhere on the mountain and tackle most of the more difficult terrain which you're likely to meet.

A frequent problem when people try fall-line turns for the first few times is that they allow the hips and shoulders to be turned in the direction of travel of the skis. The torsional effect or "block of rubber" of energy is lost and the next turn has to be started by physical force. Imagine holding a fairly large eraser rubber as if you're going to wring it. Twist the bottom half as far as it will go, then release it. It springs back. It is this kind of creation and release of energy which helps us to make effective fall-line turns. Visualise the force pulling you down the slope, from the centre of your body, and follow this line of force. You should be able to feel the skis "shooting" forward as the energy is released, so that the edge change takes place almost automatically. This effect replaces strong physical input. If there is any tendency at all to begin to force the ski at this stage, we will soon revert to the misconception that we turn the ski and then begin to try to jump the skis around, which is if nothing else quite tiring.

The pole plant often regarded as an important tool in fall-line skiing can certainly cause problems when it is badly timed. But don't get too obsessed with it. We can detract from our overall performance much more by insisting on the correct use of the pole. Feel happy with your turns first and the pole will often naturally come into use almost without you thinking about it.

Above all, don't expect too much too soon. Remember that this is a training programme and can't be hurried. Training takes place in any sport gradually, so don't rush into practising fall-line turns first thing in the morning. Have a couple of warm-up runs first, covering the progression of exercises on undemanding terrain. Only then are you ready. And at the other end of the scale, if it's just one of those days when nothing is working and you feel that you've been practising for hours to no great apparent effect, then know that it's time to stop for the day.

Skis "shooting" forward.

As you become more adventurous you may seek out greater challenges - or you may just find yourself one day on top of an unexpectedly steep part of the mountain or in breakable crust off-piste. Perhaps there is no other way to descend; or the path may be too narrow even for side slipping, that great "last resort" technique, when the alternative is blind panic. At moments like these you may realise the usefulness of being able to make very tight fall-line turns - "short swings" in professional jargon. These are probably open to more misinterpretation than most aspects of skiing.

Again, we have nothing that is really new to learn. How we apply our understanding needs to be modified to suit the demands of speed and the terrain, but remember nothing really changes. Very tight fall-line turns often appear to be an exercise in jumping the skis from side to side and indeed this is what is often taught. There is of course nothing wrong with this simply as an exercise in agility. But what you see in good short-radius turns - very active movements and rapid changes of direction, should be reactions to the demands of turning down a steep slope rather than the skier actively leaping to start the turn.

On steep slopes, there will be a degree of skid and edges need to be set sharply if we are to control our descent effectively. It is the rebound effect from the set edges which creates the impression of the skier "jumping".

The impression of the skier "jumping".

It is true that there is more physical effort required in short-swing turns. But this input is channelled purely into making sharper, stronger movements to tighten the radius of the turn and to check the end of the turn by setting the edges. Done effectively, the rebound effect is quite strong, and in effect, bounces the skier towards the fall line and into the next turn. All the effort, in other words, goes into the end of the turn, not the beginning. The rebound or the apparent "leap" is pure reaction to the more powerful forces involved. The pole is a great prop on steep slopes, so use it. It is an invaluable aid, something to lean on as the rebound take place. Do remember that you need to hold the pole quite firmly - really grip it - otherwise it will never produce the effect you want. To practise awareness of the movements needed, go back to the original exercise for the first attempts, on a moderate slope, steep enough to allow you to develop some speed, but not so much that you feel inhibited. Ski straight down the fall line, pressing the leg inwards strongly, then pause, letting the skis run up to a count of two and do the same to the other side. Resist the urge to physically turn your skies to control your speed. After the first few turns you will realise that the most secure way of achieving this is to make more progressive movements more quickly. Now experiment with shortening the pause between turns - we are aimimg for a definite and rapid change from edge to edge. Ideally, you should now find a short, quite steep slope, with a flat run-out, then practise setting the ski edges and really using the pole.

Tight fall-line turns have a nasty habit of highlighting the shortcomings in even the best performers. They demand quite energetic responses and the main problems revolve around how we react to more powerful forces on a steep slope. Excessive rotation is one common problem - the hips and shoulders swing around with the skis. To put the skis on their edges, we remember the necessary knee movements, but often forget the hip has to move in as well in a co-ordinated movement - leg lean is impossible otherwise. If you only move the knee in and don't coordinate it with the hip movement, then the result is that the hip rotates outwards and the ski is no longer on its edge.

Hip rotation is also due to not anticipating the stronger forces at the end of the turn - recall the earlier explanations. We are dealing with higher speeds, steeper terrain and stronger forces and the rhythm of movements can often go astray when you first try short turns on steep slopes. You can only learn it by practising and by not being too concerned about getting it absolutely right too soon. It is also often asking a lot of your commitment to trust what is happening when you're confronted with a steep slope, so the tendency is to force the skis around regardless, rotating physically and causing all sorts of problems, including tripping over the skis. I'm afraid there is no substitute for practice at this stage and don't forget that at this relatively advanced level, progress seems to happen more slowly than it did at the beginning.

8. bumps

There is a true story told by a friend of mine about the time he was skiing with a very famous recently-retired World Cup champion and Olympic gold medallist. They arrived at the top of a particularly nasty-looking steep field of bumps and the ex-racer stopped and shook his head. "We're not going down there," he said. "We'll go the nice way down. Bumps are for tourists". I am in complete agreement - if a bump slope is full of horrible uneven steep bumps, I feel that there is no necessity to ski them and I too will happily find another way down. You too will probably agree. Few recreational skiers can look down a field of large bumps or moguls happily. There are many perfectly legitimate reasons for this. What was a feasible bump run a couple of days after a new fall of snow may become a looming mass of squared-off monsters if it hasn't snowed for a couple of weeks, having been skied by skiers turning too quickly and not being able to follow the original line. Any line through them has long since disappeared and there is no chance of making reasonably regular turns.

Also, in these conditions, a black bumps run can actually be a very dangerous place to fall. I have seen skiers fall near the top of the black run on Toviere in Tignes, where the bumps are usually at their most fearsome and fall the whole way down, bouncing off the bumps as they go. Serious injuries can occur, so it is vital to treat this sort of run with respect. So there are good reasons that bumps are high on the list of the most disliked conditions, and to feel more than a little anxiety if there is no other way down.

Yet many skiers see the image of good bumps skiing as hurtling down the fall-line making tight turns like the free-stylers, so bump runs - particularly the steepest, nastiest ones - become a challenge. There is no doubt that a good bumps skier is an impressive sight. But how realistic is it, I ask my pupils, to ski bumps like these young, fit, fearless competitors, who do nothing but train on bumps, which themselves are artificially formed by digging them out with shovels, so that they have a perfectly regular line and are not at all like the ones we mere mortals have to ski.

To begin to understand how we can learn to cope with bumps and even enjoy them, we need to know how they were formed in the first place. Bumps are formed by us, the skiers. The passage of many pairs of turning skis carve tracks into the snow which get deeper and deeper until a perfectly manicured run, flattened by the piste machine overnight, is transformed by the end of the next day into an intimidating mass of hillocks. How big they eventually become is decided by the number of skiers, how skilful they are, the steepness of the slope and the depth and condition of the snow. It's no accident that all other things being equal, the biggest bumps appear on the steepest runs. Although that is not a thought which is likely to be very comforting if you find yourself at the top of such a slope.

The "ski-ability" of bumps is also affected by these same factors, so that if you arrive at midday after a new fall of snow on a bump slope, most reasonably effective skiers can manage quite easily. But one day later, after the ski-school classes and less skilful skiers have struggled down, the picture of the bumps looks very different. What was a good "line" the previous day has been completely altered because the round smooth bumps have become nasty, square and icy. This tends to happen because many skiers often find the existing line too committing, so they side-slip a few bumps. This squares them off, and scrapes away the snow from the downhill side so that the front of the bump becomes icy.

Several top American resorts used to have a check-point at the top of perhaps two or three selected bump fields to ensure that the standard of skiers was high enough not to destroy the line of the bumps. They used to check the length of your skis, because skis which were too short would also alter the line. This was an excellent idea, which seems to be on the decline, unfortunately. Even in the best designed modern ski resort, which offers alternative ways down the mountain, you are almost bound to be confronted with bump fields sooner or later from which there is no escape. Learning how to ski bumps is therefore an essential part of your skiing development and the result of knowing that you can get down using good basic technique means that you can even begin to enjoy them! However, as with everything we've done, effective skiing, especially as the terrain becomes more difficult, is worked on gradually, building confidence on gentle gradients. Let's look at what we already know and see how this will help us in bumps. You know already how the skis work for you and you practised tightening your turns so that you can ski in the fall line reasonable effectively on a smooth slope.

I don't expect you to start by skiing bumps in the fall line, you will be relieved to hear. But many skiers seem to think that the only way to learn to ski bumps

is by confronting the biggest, steepest bump field they can find, like the Sache in Tignes or Mont Fort in Verbier or the "Swiss Wall" in Champery, and struggling down - on some runs, there seems to be a skier stuck stationary on every other bump. All you learn by taking that approach is to be afraid.

The main priority is to remind ourselves about basics on an easy piste, preferably one that you know well. To begin our training for bumps, remember that nothing changes in basic technique - it is only modified. Warm up by doing a run working on rhythmic fall-line turns. Then do the same crouching as low as possible. Try it again, but this time stretching as high as you can. Repeat this in a mid-stance. By this time, you should have discovered that you can change the edge of the ski in almost any position and this is vital for skiing bumps well. Many pupils say that they find it helps to remember this when a nasty set of bumps appears ahead. What you are also training is the knee mobility which is essential in effective bumps skiing.

Firstly the skis can cope with moving across bumps at quite high speeds - they don't, as some people imagine, get impaled. To convince yourself of this and at the same time to build awareness of how the body needs to react in bumpy terrain, try this exercise. Find a line of friendly bumps - which means those which are just forming - perhaps four or five them across the slope. Now just traverse across them to the other side. Notice how the body reacts; the bump pushes the legs up as you move over it and then as you ski into the troughs, we should stretch the legs again. The first time you try it, you may find that you are being bounced around a bit. This is only because you're not used to the effects of moving at speed over moguls. What you're learning to do is to "flatten" the bumps, by

Try changing edges in as low a stance as possible.

"absorbing" them - you anticipate the compressing effect of the bump by allowing your legs to fold and you push back into the hollow at the other side. Stretching into the trough is a very important movement, since it allows us to maintain contact with the snow. Otherwise we can become airborne! Imagine that there is a roof which stops your head from bouncing up as you go over the bump. You press back against it as you extend into the hollow. With practice you will find that you can go quite fast in your traverse over the bumps absorbing and stretching.

You can try this with slightly steeper traverses through the bumps. Try to become familiar with the feeling of the bump pushing your legs up and you pushing back down into the hollows. Absorption or compression could be misinterpreted as "sitting back" - but all you need to remember is to try to remain over your feet - in dynamic balance. By developing awareness of how the body and skis will react perfectly naturally to undulating terrain in a traverse, we can more readily adapt what we've learned, when we want to begin to turn in bumps.

Trying to trust what the ski will do for you in long turns slowly is far more beneficial than attempting to string several short turns together quickly at this stage. Traversing through bumps, absorbing and stretching and then turning at the side and traversing across in the other direction and so on until you reach the bottom is actually a perfectly feasible way of handling bump runs and is a great way of building confidence. You can also develop an eye for where is best to make a turn during this sort of exercise. To build confidence that the ski on its edge will turn in bumpy terrain, I often ask my pupils to make these long turns across bumps, *regardless* of where the bumps are, provided of course we are on friendly terrain.

A frequent problem amongst intermediate skiers is that they try to turn too quickly in bumps. It's an understandable response to feeling intimidated by them, but is one of the worst things you can actually do. The problem is compounded because we are often told to turn by pivoting on the crest of the bump, where ski contact with the snow is minimal. The theory is that this makes it easier to turn the ski - you pivot on top and off you go down the other side. I believe that turning on the very top of the bump complicates what happen afterwards and makes the successful completion of the turn more difficult. I say this for two reasons.

For the same reason that the turn is said to be easier to start on the crest of a bump - that there is little snow contact - so it is also more difficult to stabilise the effects of the forces on us in these conditions. What typically happens is that when we set off from our pinnacle, we slither off and end up over-rotating the hips and shoulders, sometimes almost to face back uphill again, and generally feel pretty unstable. Secondly, should we try to hurry our skis through the fall line or to turn on the top of the bump, it leaves us on the steepest and most scraped part of the bump - the downhill side. If the bump is large enough, this "front" side can be almost vertical and very icy. So we land with a fairly solid thump in the troughs, again feeling rather insecure. "Pivoting" may seem to make sense if we are standing still - what happens when we are on the move is very different. If we don't turn on the crest, though, where do we turn? Look at a bump field. The downhill side of the bump (I call this the front of the bump) is usually scraped, but this snow has been deposited on the uphill side (the back) of the bump ahead. This part is also banked in our favour. These factors will make life easier.

Absorbing the bump and extending into the hollow.

Fall-line skiing in bumps

There are many different lines you can take through a bump field, as I've tried to emphasise. In the beginning, we practised long turns through a field of bumps, with perhaps quite long traverses in between. If you can do this effectively and are happy with it, there is no reason that this shouldn't be an aim in itself. You are under no obigation, after all, to ski the fall-line in bumpy terrain and many of my advanced skiers in fact find it more fun to do giant slalom-type turns. However, to be able to perform effective fall-line bumps skiing is a goal for many skiers and it is an attainable goal, providing you are fit and reasonably mobile: others should be content with slower, longer turns through bumps.

It should be clear now why I stress the importance of being able to make good fall-line turns on normal slopes - you need the degree of commitment which practising these turns gives, if you are to eventually learn to ski bumps well. However, as always, we shouldn't expect to do it immediately. Fall-line skiing in the bumps is very committing, so we build up confidence and awareness gradually. The skis and our bodies will cope, but you have to convince yourself of that. The objective here is to develop this awareness by firstly not turning at all, but by straight running. Not from the top, of course! Again find some friendly bumps, on a slope which has a good run-out (this is very important, as you will see) and ski down using the long turns you've been practising and stop perhaps three or four bumps from the bottom. Facing down the fall line, set off running straight, until you reach the bottom. Try it again until you feel confident about it, experiment with a different set of bumps, find a higher starting point, though don't become over-enthusiastic and go too high. This time, you're ready to try a few fall-line turns, again finding a starting point close to the bottom of the slope.

Think before you set off about the line you want to take. It's too late to do it on the move. Try only two or three to begin with, turning off the banked, soft snow on the bump ahead, allowing the ski to carry you round the side and into the trough. You can control your speed by making the ends of turns tighter, and allowing the contour of the bump to slow you down. An image which I've found helps many people in fall-line skiing through bumps, is to imagine that as we change edge to start the turn, the hips are aimed forwards and sideways towards the crest of the bump. This effectively projects the knees and hips towards the fall line. You recall what I said earlier, it may also help to remember that the "block of rubber" effect in fall-line skiing helps us change edge almost automatically. The contour of the bump also helps us change edge. The bump compresses the legs, the skis carry you through the fall line and into the trough and it is here that you push back against the edged ski, to extend into the hollow.

Accomplished bumps skiers can change edge whilst they're compressed, to ensure a sharp and precise start to the next turn. Perhaps you remember the exercises I asked you to do, crouching as low as possible, and making fall-line turns in that position? Now you can see why it is a useful form of practice for bumps skiing. People get the impression that good bumps skiers "sit back" during the compression. Again this is a misinterpretation. In bumps, the impetus of hitting a bump tends to throw us forward and our natural reaction is to maintain dynamic balance, creating the appearance of "sitting back". It is the result of reactions to moving over bumps, not a "sitting back" action.

By this time if you feel reasonably confident about your progress, try starting your fall-line turns from higher up the slope, working on committed and positive movements. You may have found that you are using your poles without even thinking about it. If so, that's good. However, many people when they try fall-line bumps skiing initially, find that they get into a tangle with their poles. As before, I feel strongly that you shouldn't worry about precisely where to plant the poles. Most often, this tends to happen naturally as a result of getting everything else right and specific instructions aren't helpful in any event, because there are several factors to be taken into account, such as arm length, pole length and terrain. Just remember not to block your direction of travel with the poles.

As in any committed fall-line skiing, effective pole work can be of enormous help in bumps. Done well, it helps to stabilise the upper body so that we can keep facing down the fall line and use the torsional build-up of energy to its full advantage. At the same time, it gives us something to lean on as we change edge. You also have to remember that you're moving forward as you plant the pole, so really work on stiffening the arm as the pole hits the snow, thus "riding over" it. Feeble pole plants won't help in bumps! Good rhythm and timing are crucial, but again this is only something that you can develop through practice. It cannot be taught.

There will, of course, be problems. You have to expect to fall, maybe quite often, when you're learning about bumps skiing, which is one of the

A good pole plant helps to stabilise the upper body.

reasons I emphasise training on gentler slopes where falling over doesn't matter so much.

One of the most frequent problems in skiing bumps is "over-rotation". This means that the upper body has swung round, the hips rotate outwards, instead of leaning to the centre of the turn, the ski loses its edge and over you go, usually backwards. What is responsible for over-rotation can in itself be due to several factors.

One cause is trying to turn too quickly. In our enthusiasm to get through the dreaded fall line as soon as possible, we force the skis around using physical rotation. The inside ski catches for the same reason - we push the turning ski towards the fall line and the inside edge of the other one "hooks" us around, rotating the body even more. Another reason could be our failure to anticipate what I call the "stopping effect" of the bump. As we reach the back of the next bump, especially at speed, this stopping effect tends to create strong rotation, unless we stabilise the upper body by using the arms and a good solid pole plant. I sometimes ask my pupils to feel that they are really exaggerating stretching out their arms in front of them as stabilisers - and then by doing this, they are actually adopting a normal position for fall-line skiing. Remember just because something feels exaggerated or strange, doesn't mean that it isn't right. Ineffective use of the poles can be another cause of over-rotation. If you forget to stiffen the arm at the moment of impact, the jolt will bend the arm backwards, turning the shoulders and the hips around with it. A frequent problem in bumps skiing is gathering too much speed. Two factors are responsible for control. One is the stopping effect already mentioned, which providing you anticipate it, will help you control your speed, because that part of the bump is banked already in your favour. (Hence the importance of choosing the right line.) The second means of control is by tightening the radius of the turn. This means thinking of "fish-hooks" - tightening the end of the turn.

Don't forget that no two bump slopes are the same and the same slope can change dramatically within a day, so you should vary your line through the bumps to suit your ability, fitness and mental state. And you shouldn't become too obsessed with perfecting your fall-line bumps turns to the exclusion of everything else. I hardly ever ski the fall line in bumps when I am out for a day's free skiing, preferring to make long, fast turns instead. Confidence will come from the knowledge that what works for you in normal terrain will also work on more difficult slopes. Accept that it will take time and lots of training before a field of large bumps will lose its ogerish quality and seem quite friendly instead. Some bumps never do, even to me, so don't feel inadequate if you sometimes feel afraid. I have never lost what I think is a healthy respect for some very steep bump slopes. You will notice how much importance I place on training on terrain that doesn't have menacing bumps. You cannot learn on slopes which frighten you, so don't be persuaded to attempt something which is really beyond you. I think that it is a good idea to pause sometimes, and take stock of how much progress you have already made. Once you have refined and practised your technique sufficiently to have become a reasonably effective bumps skier, you will find that the possibilities of where you can ski are that much more open and that is worth the struggle in itself.

9. ice

A fact of skiing life is that ice is something which is sooner or later unavoidable. It is partly caused by that sunshine, which we all love, melting the snow, which freezes at night and turns to ice by morning. Also we, the skiers, contribute by packing the snow down hard, and scraping the snow cover with the frequent passes of edges until the piste is honed and gleaming. Even a normal piste, which on a Spring morning can resemble rock-hard corduroy after the piste-bashing machines have done their work the night before, can produce a teeth-jarring ride until the sun softens the snow and this can be just as unnerving to ski on as true ice. Ice in itself can be tricky enough, but as pistes become busier each season, skiing on an icy piste with other skiers is positively hazardous. The sooner we can learn to cope with it, therefore, the better, even if we never actually learn to enjoy it.

To me, ice is an extreme example of some of the difficulties that you may ordinarily face as soon as you ski on hard-packed snow. Excessive skidding happens more readily in these conditions, so you feel very insecure. On ice, these effects are intensified. The problem is compounded by the body reacting defensively - tensing the muscles, stiffening the joints and generally making life difficult. Cramp in the feet is often a sure sign of tenseness - toes gripping the soles of the boots frantically trying to hang on. The very sound-effects of skiing on ice are intimidating: scraping, rasping noises which alert you to be on guard.

To understand these problems we must look again at the effects of friction. We take this so much for granted in everyday life that we don't even think about how we walk or run, we just do it. Indeed, in many activities in which our bodies receive feedback through friction we can reach a reasonable level of competence with little or no formal coaching. Remember how it feels when you are walking along the street in winter and you suddenly step on a patch of ice? As we said at the very beginning, the influence of friction is considerably reduced, you slide, the body gets less feedback, becomes confused and you fall over.

When you ski you are always on a sliding base, but we have seen how you can learn to overcome this inherent fact by using the design of the ski to work for you to produce positive feedback. If you revert to starting the turn by physical input - which makes the skis skid even more on ice - the body gets very confused feedback indeed.

In softer snow, the effects of this are less noticeable because there is more resistance to the ski skidding sideways. The skis will, in these conditions, easily work for us (even if we haven't been taught how to use them to our advantage) and so the body receives enough information to be able to respond with reasonable effectiveness.

On ice, there is little resistance to the skis skidding, especially if we force them around. So what should we do? You often hear that you should be "more aggressive", "attack" or "fight" the mountain. To me, nothing could be less appropriate to skiing in general, and is particularly inappropriate to skiing on ice.

Again, our basic technique doesn't change. Allow

Commited, precise, but **gentle** changes of edge are
needed on ice.

the skis to run on their edges; use them as they were designed to be used, to turn you, and you will find that the degree of sideways skid, which causes your problems on ice, is reduced. Commit yourself at the beginning of the turn to edge change, but do so *gently*. Soft but progressive movements are needed. Think of skiing in curves. The movements *must be soft* because any physically strong movement will only produce excessive skidding in these conditions. The movements *must be progressive*, because this helps control. The more softly and precisely we can change edge at the beginning of the turn, the greater the chance of control at the end. Physical force, on ice, will only make you feel less secure than ever. Think instead of skiing on eggs; any hard movements and they will break.

You also sometimes hear that you should "put more weight on your downhill ski" when skiing on ice. If you already have started to skid, then physically putting more weight on the skidding ski doesn't help. Remember weight distribution on skis is a result of the forces that are set up by us travelling at speed in the turn and the positions we need to adopt to react to them. If you try to put more weight on one ski, you will lose the edge that you need to keep control. Having said all of this, I would not expect to ski very well on ice either, unless my skis were able to do the job. You don't need to buy a special pair of skis. Good models are now being designed to cope in all conditions. Whatever skis you have, it is essential that for skiing on ice, their edges should be sharp, to give the "grip" which will help you.

10. powder

The classic dream of most skiers is a vision of skiing through untracked deep snow in the sunshine, casting sparkling plumes of fluffy powder upwards and feeling as if you're floating on a cloud. But many recreational skiers have convinced themselves that this is a dream which never comes true. "Skiing the powder" well is often portrayed as the mark of distinction which sets the experts apart from the rest. But I believe that having reached this point, almost any recreational skier can learn to cope well with deeper snow, by applying what we have already discovered. However, there are many misunderstandings and psychological inhibitions which can cause problems before we even set off into deep snow.

Sometimes we feel apprehensive. Despite the images of soft, light-as-air snow, many people are afraid of venturing into it. It may be fear of the unknown - the "what if" factor. Not being able to see one's skis, or what lies under the snow can also have inhibiting effects. Fear of speed and of falling compound the apprehension. Add to these the many misconceptions about technique for skiing in powder snow and it isn't surprising that so many skiers get discouraged. There are some very firmly held views in different quarters about how we should ski powder and often the misconceptions come about because you're often told that the technique for skiing deep snow is different. For instance, if you watch an effective skier coming towards you through deep snow, the visual impression can be completely misleading. You see the feet and legs apparently being pushed from side to side. Indeed, this is often taught.

In normal piste conditions, the skis can skid sideways, so it is possible to simulate this on packed down snow. In deep snow, if your concept of turning is to push the skis sideways in a physically-induced skid, it won't work because there is resistance to this sideways movement, which is why many skiers have difficulties in these conditions and so they are taught to jump the skis in deep snow.

Look at the tracks left by effective skiers in soft snow; they are curves or "S" shapes - the skis follow their length, *carrying* the feet from side to side. This is what is responsible for our impression of the feet being "pushed" from side to side. But if we really were pushing the feet sideways, the tracks left would look completely different from an 'S'. They would resemble say, a series of windscreen wiper tracks down the slope.

Another misconception about powder-snow skiing is that you should "sit back". It is an impression which

Classic tracks in powder.

when copied is responsible for much fatigue and painful thigh muscles. What is responsible for the "sitting back" impression can be explained by the pictures here.

In contrast to what happens on a hard-packed slope, in deep snow when the skis move at speed, the tips tend to come up to the surface - they begin to "plane". It is this effect which creates the illusion of the skier actively trying to sit back. Again, it is a reaction, in this case to speed in deep snow and is

not primarily a physically-induced action by the skier. It may be necessary in certain circumstances, which depend on the depth and the consistency of the snow and the gradient of the slope, to very slightly adjust your weight backwards to begin with in order to overcome the resistance of the snow and to allow you to gather speed. This allows the skis to plane to the surface. But thereafter it is a question of remaining in dynamic balance. As usual, a static interpretation of what happens when we are moving will not help our skiing.

Other instructions about skiing in deep snow tell you to put your weight evenly on both feet. As with many things in skiing, this is another example of an observation of a reaction, which is then analysed and taught as an action. In deep snow, there is no firm base and as we turn, the resultant force creates fairly even pressure over both skis. It is not necessary to think about actively doing this - it will happen as a result of the forces in the turn. I would like to add here that I believe these considerations only come into play in very deep snow, the "bottomless powder" of exceptional conditions.

You are also told to keep your feet together in deep snow. The reason given is that the snow will separate the skis so that they cross or otherwise get

into a tangle. But if your skis are wandering off in different directions, then something is going wrong in basic technique. For instance starting off in too wide a stance or a defensive sitting down stance, both of which make it difficult to angulate sufficiently. No amount of forcing the feet together will cure the underlying problem, which has to be addressed first.

First steps in deep snow

Our mental images of deep snow skiing conjure up pictures of effortlessness and grace, but you cannot copy these. What you can do, though, is to copy what creates what you see. As you progress, it is also worth remembering that your mental commitment will be tested as you move into unfamiliar territory. This is why it is important not to over-complicate things, especially when you first venture into deep snow. As we have said, powder skiing, in particular, suffers from an unnecessary mystique about "special technique". As in everything else I've explained, what we learn at the beginning does not change as we become more advanced. Sound basic technique only needs slight modification to allow us to adapt to new challenges of terrain and snow conditions. There is no doubt that the sensation of skiing in deep snow is very different from skiing on prepared pistes and it takes time to get used to this alone.

There are many ways to enjoy skiing in deep snow. As with bumps skiing, you don't have to ski down the steepest slopes in the fall line, nor do you even have to be a particularly good fall-line skier, though it helps. To me, to this day, one of the greatest pleasures in skiing is to just run straight or traverse through deep snow.

To appreciate what does happen in powder snow skiing, we have to bear in mind that the skis will work for us in deep snow as they did in other conditions. Hitherto, we have needed greater speed to get through deep snow, since it is speed which provides the energy required to help the skis work. And this is perhaps the very thing which many who are just beginning to learn to ski powder don't want to do. Modern ski technology has come to the rescue in this respect for newcomers to powder - and for old hands alike, I might add. Because the modern ski has greater side-cut than ever before, spread over a wider but shorter area of ski, it enables us to perform the movements necessary to ski in deep snow without having to ski faster. Many teachers nowadays in fact will only ski with their classes off-piste if the pupils are using the deeper side-cut skis, so helpful are they to better performance.

Beginning to cope with powder, however, can be

approached in the same way as we have done before - experimenting gradually with what we already know will work for us, in different situations. If you are lucky enough, you may wake up one morning to a covering of powder snow on the pistes and then is the best time to get out early and play with all of our earlier exercises. Straight running or traversing are excellent ways to develop a feeling for deeper snow and I cannot emphasise how important this is. To appreciate that the sensation *is different from* skiing on hard packed snow though needs time. Take a dive into it. Deliberately falling around in soft snow may seem like a second childhood, but it helps us to lose some of our fears about skiing in powder. Try running from the piste into the soft snow off to the sides and back again, feeling the slowing down and the acceleration. Please, however, *never* leave the marked ski run area on you own or with inexperienced skiers.

Learning to turn in deep snow involves no mystery. The first sensations may seem different but you shouldn't mistake this as a signal that you need to ski differently. To show that the ski will still work for you as usual, we work through the first exercises, especially the edge and angulation exercises. At this stage, as you may have already noticed, you should also be prepared to fall, perhaps quite a lot. If you think of falling in deep snow, losing skis, getting covered in snow and so on as a nuisance, then as I sometimes say to my pupils, you will have problems! Pupils have often said that despite first attempts, when every turn one way seems to be accompanied by a fall in the other direction, the frustration was more than made up for by the turns when everything was right and they felt that they understood what I meant when I said that "nothing changes". When I take people into deep snow for their first few runs, I ask them to use long radius

turns, pushing the leg in with the hand to remind them to edge the ski. Long turns are less committing and give you more time to think. These exercises by now will seem very familiar, even elementary, but remember that familiar exercises are just what we need to rely on in unfamiliar territory.

Resist the urge to turn the skis by physical force. If you do, you won't succeed. Once the ski is on its edge, it is *most* important to *allow the ski to run into the fall-line.*

This will seem to take a long time in comparison to skiing on the piste. As a result, there is often the desire to hurry the turn, with attempts to force the ski around and turning the body into the turn, all of which end in tears. Trust the ski to turn. It does take an act of faith that if edge and angulation exercises worked on the piste, so they will work in deeper snow. If you practise at slower speeds to begin with, you will soon gain the confidence to allow the skis to run faster. This speed will help you to turn.

As you ski faster, you will notice more that at the end of every turn there is a kind of "stopping" effect as the force makes the skis sink into the snow. Because the skis cannot go sideways through deep snow, the "stopping" effect on us is greater and we need to resist it more, to stop it from pulling us over. It is extremely important to anticipate this and it is *vital* to keep the hips well into the centre of the turn. Some pupils say that they really *exaggerate* "reaching out" to help them produce the necessary amount of angulation. You then of course, must remember that to start the next turn, you need to rise to a neutral position, otherwise you end up lower and lower, completely blocking the required range of movement.

Fall-line skiing in powder

If you can ski effective fall-line turns on hard packed snow, you should be able to adapt what you have learned to powder snow quite easily. There are a few things to be prepared for, however, which may unsettle you until you become more familiar with the sensations of skiing the fall line in powder snow. Be aware in particular that the force pulling you to the outside of the turn in deeper snow feels much greater than on piste and you must become used to allowing for this. If you can recall when you first practised fall-line skiing, the forces that are generated actually help us to perform more effectively if you learn how to harness them to your advantage. Remember that good skiers make it look effortless because they use the existing forces to their advantage. The "block of rubber" effect, I think is an important image to keep in mind.

The faster we travel, the greater are the forces in the turn. In deep snow, this means that the pressure exerted by these forces on the skis makes the skis sink further into the snow. The body crosses the line of travel of the skis at the end of the turn and the release of pressure changes edges for us almost automatically. Just as we needed to anticipate the effects of the forces in bumps skiing, so we should be ready for similar effects in deep snow. The feeling of the skis "shooting forward" is again, as it was in bumps skiing, a *reaction* to what is happening. If you watch an accomplished powder-snow skier swooping downhill, it is easy to misinterpret this pure reaction as a direct physical action by the skier. The feeling is that the skis shoot forwards towards the fall line and to the surface of the snow, with a considerable degree of impetus if we are travelling fast. This produces what is sometimes referred to as a "bouncing" feeling. and is what is responsible for the misconception that we

jump the skis to turn in powder snow.

As we saw, in bumps skiing we absorb the force created by hitting a bump and allow the legs to compress during the edge change and then extend the legs during the turn. So, as the snow gets deeper, and we ski steeper slopes or simply go faster, the force at the end of the turn pulls us further into the snow. This creates a "sinking" effect. As we initiate our next turn, and move towards the fall line, the skis will rise to the surface. The force of the skis coming to the surface should be absorbed by letting the legs compress and then extending them against the edges to complete the turn. If you could look at a profile of our tracks through the snow, it is almost like looking at a series of bumps. In fact, as we ski faster in deep snow, this is exactly how it should be treated. The end result is an impression of effortlessness, but is caused by you, the skier, harnessing the working of the ski and the energy which comes from speed to your advantage. Effective use of the poles does help, but I can only remind you that it shouldn't become a fixation to the detriment of your skiing. I know many good powder-snow skiers who don't rely upon a strong pole plant in these conditions.

What can go wrong

The prepared pistes are always there ready and waiting for us to ski them. Unfortunately, we have to wait for the right opportunity to ski in powder snow, and even when it falls in the right quantities, we will often have to wait until it becomes safe to ski. So we don't always have as much practice time in deep snow, and therefore progress is inevitably slower than you would wish (unless you are one of those relatively rare holiday skiers who take to it like a duck to water). This is one of the first problems. Luckily, this is becoming less of a problem than it used to be due to the advent of the deeper side cut ski, which in my experience vastly reduces the time taken to become an effective powder snow skier. The confidence to speed up develops quickly and this alone helps us to overcome the problems we may face in skiing powder. Like anything else, however, you have to build up gradually and not expect too much until you become accustomed to the different experience of powder-snow skiing.

There are other more specific problems which you may find are inhibiting your progress. They may have several, interlocking causes, but some of the more common problems encountered are easily identified. How often have you fallen in deep snow, with the skis crossed? The source of this problem is often trying to force the skis to turn into the fall line; the body rotates to turn the skis by force, the turning ski is therefore pushed ahead of the other ski and then they both cross, and over you go. Even if we succeed in getting through the fall line, forcing the ski around may also result in the inside ski hooking and sends us spiralling backwards to the outside of the turn. This is one of the commonest of all deep snow falls. I emphasise commitment as part of the solution, because it helps us to remember to trust that the ski will turn us if it is on its edge and we are ready to respond - providing that you don't try to *rush* the turn. Edge (push the leg towards the fall-line for the first turn to remind you) then *pause* to *allow* the ski to run into the fall-line. I cannot emphasise this enough. Do you remember what I said earlier about concepts of turning? My bindings are set at the lowest setting possible in all conditions and speeds - if my concept of turning was to rotate the ski around, I would twist out of the bindings at every turn!

The old habit of shifting weight is another problem in deep-snow skiing. As we have observed so often before, if you try physically to transfer pressure on to the turning ski, it will flatten and sink into the snow. This will either rotate us around out of our bindings, or take us off down the slope at some speed, since *flat skis don't turn*. As the ski is not on its edge, you can't resist the sideways force and so it pulls you to the outside of the turn and again, over you go.

It is worth remembering that many difficulties in skiing, not just in deep snow, are due to our lack of awareness of the effects of the forces set up in the turn. To go back to basics for a moment, any heavy object travelling at speed in a curve is subjected to a force to the outside of that curve. On hard-packed snow, where the ski sinks into the snow very little, the force pulling us outwards means for most of us a greater degree of sideways movement. But in deep snow, that sideways motion - the skid - is largely prevented by the depth of the snow resisting it, and so the effect of the force, at the end of the turn especially, is more pronounced. To understand this properly, you only have to look at where most falls in powder snow happen - to the outside of the turn, leaving us rather inelegantly pinned on our backs. What causes this rotation is the effect of the force pulling our hips (the centre of mass of the body) outwards. This is why angulation must be exaggerated when skiing deep snow It is only

through adequate "leg lean" - hips and legs leaning lying to the centre of the turn that we can resist the force.

There are other inhibitions which we can suffer in powder snow, some of which we have already touched upon, like not being able to see your skis. Training ourselves to trust that as long as the ski tracking through the snow on its edge in a curve, it will turn us, is the surest cure I know for this problem. Another less obvious feature of deep-snow skiing is that it will not always take place in brilliant sunshine and perfect visibility. Occasionally, that untracked paradise can be encountered in heavy snowfalls and hence poor visibility. Everyone withdraws to some extent when the weather deteriorates and it is quite sensible to slow down and be cautious. Don't go to the top of the mountain in these conditions. We tend to head for areas below the tree line in these conditions,so that you have some horizons to fix upon, so you aren't skiing blind, as it were. Again I can only say that effective technique learned from a basic level is the most secure defence. Awareness that the ski will work for you regardless of bad light and difficult terrain has helped many people. You may think it is perverse, but I consider that skiing in poor conditions actually helps me to maintain my standard of skiing.

11. safety off-piste

To experience the very special pleasure of skiing in the winter wilderness of the mountains is the dream of many skiers. It is perhaps their ultimate goal. And as resorts become busier every year, more and more skiers are deserting the pistes for the great open spaces which lie in the distance. "Off-piste" can mean skiing within a few yards of the runs or venturing further afield. (Ski touring is in its own category, involving extensive mileage and days and nights spent high up in the mountains.) However near or far you go off-piste, the attraction which these mountain areas has for skiers seems to be magnetic. We still have the freedom to roam the mountains. It is a freedom which we must treasure since it is one which is legally denied in some countries. But it is also a freedom with rules attached and these rules must be respected. Nowadays there are more than just a few people who risk their own and other's lives by being ignorant of these rules or - and this is unforgivable - just ignoring them. Every winter someone somewhere becomes a victim of an avalanche and joins the tragic list of statistics, made more so by the realisation that the incident could nearly always have been avoided . There are the skiers who have been caught in avalanches because their friends went down the same slope the day before or that morning or even last year and said that it was "safe".... There are the snow boarders who simply don't differentiate between piste and off-piste and so go regardless. The list could go on. The rules are easy to learn.

All ski resorts have ski patrols - highly trained men and women - whose primary task is to ensure the safety of the pistes for those who venture into their domain. Every day they assess snow conditions and weather forecasts in order to determine avalanche risk. In glacial areas this includes assessment of the snow covering crevasses. They will produce a snow profile and give specific information on avalanche risk according to an international scale. The level of risk is given a number indicating the percentage likelihood of avalanches occuring that day. This information is printed on notices in the tourist office and at the patrol headquarters and most resorts have large noticeboards giving piste information including avalanche risk. So there really is no excuse for not knowing. Do familiarise yourself with the warnings - and heed them.

The patrols will close some marked runs too if there is general avalanche danger, so look around you to check. Generalised avalanche danger is usually indicated by the flying of a black flag at strategic points around the resort. There are also ropes and signs warning us when we are about to leave the marked and patrolled ski area.

It is, unfortunately, not unusual for skiers to take off into unmarked areas in complete ignorance of mountain dangers and with little awareness of what might befall them. My advice is to only go off-piste with those who are qualified to take you there - mountain guides who spend years studying and training before they achieve their qualification, or professional, fully-qualified ski teachers, who also have additional training and mountain experience

off-piste. This does not mean party leaders, perhaps supplied by tour operators or ski clubs, or teachers with lesser qualifications. A properly organised group will also have the necessary equipment which it is essential to take, including avalanche "bleepers" and shovels. The bleeper is in fact a transceiver designed to locate victims of avalanches buried under the snow. It is almost universal practice for groups going off-piste to be issued with these by the ski teacher, and they should also, of course, give you a training session in how to use them. We have a weekly practice with off-piste groups, in the use of bleepers and everyone gets the chance to perfom a search.

It should go without saying that it is suicidal to go off-piste alone, as the records of the piste patrols annually show. Beware also friends claiming a little experience. If all of this seems dramatic, then it is said with the knowledge that if the joys of skiing off the beaten track are easy to see, then its dangers are equally real, if less obvious, because they lurk in wait for the unaware. I would like to remind you of the sobering thought voiced by a mountain guide friend of mine, that the more one skis off-piste the greater the probability of one day being caught in an avalanche.

Off-piste equipment

The modern ski, with its deep side-cut, can be used for both piste and off-piste skiing, and there are some excellent all-round skis on the market, so unless you want to,you don't actually need a special pair. There are, however skis which are designed to be used more off-piste and most manufacturers produce a range to choose from should you decide that is what you want. Specific off-piste skis certainly make life easier for the less skilful skier.

The other bits of equipment which are important especially off-piste, include double lens goggles, together with a pocket full of tissues and supplemented by a tube of good anti-mist. Many people have an utterly miserable time because they have inadequate eye protection in these conditions. It also helps, should you be wearing sun glasses, that they are attached to you in some way with a strap, in case you go powder-diving. It is almost impossible to find sunglasses lost in deep snow. Clothing too matters in deep-snow skiing. One-piece suits are preferable to a jacket and trousers since they have fewer places where snow can get inside and down your trouser leg. Long-cuffed gloves are better than short ones and are more comfortable.

...and losing it

This is another aspect of deep-snow skiing that deserves a special mention. If you go to a ski resort in springtime, after the snow has melted, you would probably be amazed at the number of ski poles and lone skis found in areas where people have skied in deep snow during winter, not to mention other diverse bits and pieces. Falling in deep snow can be a very frustrating experience if in doing so you lose your skis, poles and other equipment and don't know the correct way of looking for them. There is, yes, a correct method. Skis are obviously the most important things to locate, since it is a serious matter if you have to walk out of a powder field. It is also not wise to hang around sitting in the middle of a powder field for too long, so it is also important to find the lost ski as quickly as possible.

There is a set routine to follow for finding lost skis in deep snow and it should be adhered to religiously. Check that you are in one piece and don't try to leap up immediately. Find out what is missing. It's unusual to lose both skis and poles, so there is often one of them at hand to help you in the next stage. Feel around you carefully in case the missing equipment is nearby. I emphasise *carefully* here, since if you jump up and start thrashing around like most people do, the chances are that you will end up burying whatever is lost for good, or at least until springtime. Failing that, look at your tracks before you go any further, and try to remember where you fell. You can often tell from the snow. Falls off-piste can be quite spectacular and skis can end up surprisingly far away.

If you have friends around, organise them into a line abreast and, starting at least 10 - 20 metres below where you fell, get them to "slice" the snow in a criss-cross section with the heel of a ski. A ski, once released from its binding, can travel in a straight line quite a long way under the snow because the stoppers don't work and can also come to rest on its side, so it is important to be thorough and give yourself a good margin of error.

It is very useful to wear long, fluorescent nylon cords (available at all ski shops), with one end attached to your binding and the other stuffed up your trouser leg. They are long enough, when deployed, to rise to the surface of the snow and in the event that the snow is deeper than the length of the tape, they can still be seen glowing through the snow, pointing the way to your ski! This could save a lot of time and inconvenience, not to say potential danger from getting stuck on a mountain side without your skis.

Getting up after a fall is also not quite as simple as it is on hard snow. The snow tends to fall away from you with every movement and you sink further into it. Try to pack the snow down around you to make a more stable platform from which you can put on your skis. Don't be in a hurry. If you flounder around trying to reattach your equipment too quickly, you will only as likely as not fall over again. As you might have noticed, getting up in powder snow is quite tiring. Once you are up, do remember to clear all the packed snow away from the sole of your boot before putting on your ski again. A useful trick is to dig the heel of the ski into the snow at a slight upward angle so that the binding does not get covered again in snow.

12. fitness and the skiing environment

There are things which can stand in the way of your progress before you even put on your skis; the effects of being in the mountains; being unprepared - this covers many possibilities; not being physically fit, having unsuitable equipment, our existing ideas about what is good skiing, fear of various kinds. The list is almost endless. You may experience some or all of these and could add to the list other things, no doubt. Let's look at a few of the factors and see how they can inhibit our skiing and what we can do about them.

Skiers are often first attracted to skiing by its image in the holiday brochures, of blue skies and sunshine. But skiing is a mountain sport. This can and often does mean strong winds, snow and extreme cold. I have heard many skiers complaining when it snows, as if it is spoiling their holiday. I'm afraid I am not very sympathetic to this attitude. It is precisely this "bad" weather which makes it possible to ski in the first place. You don't get very much skiing time if you wait only for the good days, so if you want to get the most out of your holiday, you should be prepared to encounter snow, poor visibility, cold and chill winds, as well as the beautiful sunlit days.

If you have skied for more than a few seasons, you will almost certainly have experienced the alarming way in which the mountain weather can alter within a few hours or even minutes. I've spent years in ski resorts and learned to watch for signs of approaching bad weather, but unless you have special training, I don't expect most people to have the experience to do this. However, it pays to be aware of what you can be confronted with and to learn to expect the unexpected.

You will be better prepared for skiing if you learn about the inhibiting and, at worst, dangerous effects of cold and wind chill. Skiers frequently make the mistake of supposing that because the weather down in the village is still and warm, that the same will be true higher up on the ski slope. Temperatures on average fall by about 1 degree Centigrade for every 150 metres rise in altitude. This means that, at a conservative estimate, you can generally expect the temperature up on the slopes to be at least 10 degrees colder than in the resort itself. There are other factors to consider too. Even if the air is calm, at 0 degrees Centigrade (quite warm for the Alpine winter), moving at quite slow to average speeds in skiing, up to 24 k.p.h., can have a considerable cooling effect on the body. Add to this lower air temperatures and a stiff breeze, and unless skiers are properly protected, there is increasing danger from frost-bite.

What to wear is not, therefore, just a matter of fashion on the slopes - it is a vital barrier between you and the elements. You need clothes which will keep you warm and dry, if you want to ski in all conditions. To achieve this, it is important to have ski clothing which is waterproof and windproof. It used to be difficult finding clothes which were both and which felt comfortable to wear. Nowadays, you are spoiled for choice, with a large range of high-tech all-weather ski suits. If you are a keen skier, who braves all the elements, it is worth investing in a good one.

The same comment applies to just about any other piece of ski gear. Having acquired all the necessary equipment, at the risk of sounding frivolous, it is important not to leave it in your hotel room. I am amazed at the number of skiers who arrive at the for their class having left - not forgotten - goggles, hats, jackets and so on. They say "I didn't think I'd need them...." Then the blizzard starts when you're miles away from anywhere.

Fitness

Another factor which can seriously limit our skiing performance is our state of physical fitness. Skiing is a particularly dynamic sport that is performed in a highly demanding environment. But down in the cities modern life invites us to be sedentary. In other societies and times, our physical condition was important for basic survival. Nowadays, we have to make a special effort to incorporate fitness programmes into our daily lives. However, there is no real excuse, other than sheer slothfulness, for not doing something about our physical condition, giving the plethora of books, magazines, videos, television programmes and training courses devoted to the subject and every town with several gyms and swimming pools.

"Getting fit" however is a vague phrase in itself. Not even the specialists agree on exactly what it means. But it does make sense to talk about fitness for something. The best trained track athletes in the world, for instance, would not necessarily be fit in the right way for other sports. Skiing makes special demands on our level of physical fitness. Try a fairly ordinary exercise such as running up a flight of stairs. Then attempt running down the same stairs. What you notice is that whilst you ran out of breath more easily going up, you felt a different kind of fatigue on the way back down - the stress was felt particularly in the leg muscles. Running downstairs illustrates the kind of reactive strength which you need when you ski. Few activities make similar demands in this respect. Add to this the unaccustomed effects of altitude and cold temperatures on performance and you can see why skiing requires special preparation. There is no doubt that you will get more out of your precious week's holiday if you train yourself properly, yet in this age of the health and fitness boom, I am still surprised by the number of people who set off for the mountains physically ill-prepared.

Not only does this mean that they often spend the first couple of days nursing sore limbs, but also they stand greater risk of injury to muscles and joints. What you're training is progressive conditioning to the demands of skiing. During exercise your rate of breathing goes up because you need more oxygen than you do when you're resting. But have you noticed how much harder you have to breathe when you are at altitude? This is the body's way of getting the oxygen it needs from the thinner air of the mountains.

To help prepare your system as efficiently as possible for this, a general fitness programme should be the first priority. The benefits reach far beyond improving your physical condition alone. Recent university studies of different ways of training came to a thought-provoking conclusion. The most commonly-felt benefit was the least quantifiable, but the most tangible in the minds of the guinea-pigs. They all said that they simply felt better. Their general awareness of well-being was vastly improved. But to be of real value, your general fitness programme ideally should become part of your way of life. Whatever activity you choose, it should be something you can enjoy. There are many alternatives.

Running and walking are some of the most natural forms of human exercise. They are also some of the least expensive. Your only outlay is a good pair of trainers. But if you are really unfit, then you can't begin with an athlete's training schedule. You must literally walk before you can run. Remember that you can start by leaving the car at home. There are many good specialised books which will advise you how to go about building up your running or jogging programme, so do consult them.

You can incorporate skiing-orientated exercises into your daily run in order to build awareness of skiing positions and movements. You can run slowly down hills, to build reactive strength and can practice angulation positions and movements by pulling against fences or leaning on trees! In any form of training, there is less incentive to do it if boredom sets in, so it is useful to vary your programme with alternatives.

Hill-walking is an excellent way of getting fit, and puts less stress on the joints and shins. You will need to walk at a reasonable pace for a longer period of time than you would if you went for a run, to get the same fitness benefits, but many people prefer it. It is also inherently interesting, so you don't get bored.

A well earned rest half way up a ridge on the Black Cullin range, Skye.

Another sport - often as my main form of exercise - is cycling. It is easier than most to incorporate into the day's timetable, because you can use it as transport. Cycling will improve general fitness as well as increasing leg strength. It is often regarded as one of the best forms of exercise for skiing. We actually use mountain bikes because you can get away from cars and roads and away into the countryside. The mountain bike can add much the enjoyment of being in the mountains, covering forest roads, ridges and high passes in summer. Cycling in hilly terrain is excellent fitness training for skiing. This is where I think mountain bikes come into their own, because they will happily cope with tracks and rough roads that would be difficult for less sturdy bicycles. You may well have your own favourite sport or type of exercise that you can adapt in a way which is suitable for ski-fitness.

However you do it, fitness training will reward you several times over for the initial effort. Skiing also means that we need to extend our range of movements, making them more precise and swift, to enable us to react to the forces set up when we move downhill. To do this well, we require flexibility, agility and strength as well as overall fitness. These abilities are partly inborn, but can be improved enormously with practice. For instance, children have a huge advantage in flexibility, and although this tends to deteriorate as we get older, if we keep active we can maintain flexibility through exercises. However, consult a specialist for advice if you have had a recent or recurring injury before starting on any new exercise programme. Start slowly to begin with, whatever type of exercise you choose, if you're unaccustomed to it. Gradual development of training is not only the safest way, but also produces the most long lasting results.

Wind Chill Chart

Wind or skiing speed (km/h)	Temperature (°C)																		
	10	7	4	2	-1	-4	-7	-9	-12	-15	-18	-21	-23	-26	-29	-32	-34	-37	-40
	Effective temperature (°C)																		
Wind still	10	7	4	2	-1	-4	-7	-9	-12	-15	-18	-21	-23	-26	-29	-32	-34	-37	-40
6 - 12	10	7	2	-1	-4	-7	-9	-12	-15	-18	-21	-23	-26	-29	-32	-34	-37	-40	-42
13 - 19	4	2	-1	-7	-9	-12	-15	-18	-23	-26	-29	-32	-37	-40	-42	-46	-51	-54	-57
20 - 28	2	-1	-4	-9	-12	-18	-21	-23	-29	-32	-34	-40	-42	-46	-51	-54	-57	-62	-65
29 - 36	-1	-4	-7	-12	-15	-18	-23	-26	-32	-34	-37	-42	-46	-51	-54	-59	-62	-65	-71
37 - 42	-1	-4	-9	-12	-18	-21	-26	-29	-34	-37	-42	-46	-51	-54	-59	-62	-68	-71	-76
43 - 52	-1	-7	-12	-15	-18	-23	-29	-32	-34	-40	-46	-48	-54	-57	-62	-65	-71	-73	-79
53 - 60	-4	-9	-12	-15	-21	-23	-29	-34	-37	-40	-46	-51	-54	-59	-62	-68	-73	-76	-82
61 - 67	-4	-12	-12	-18	-21	-26	-29	-34	-37	-42	-48	-51	-57	-59	-65	-71	-73	-79	-82

☐ No real danger to a properly clothed skier

☐ Danger - exposed skin would freeze in approximately one minute

☐ Great danger - exposed skin would freeze in approximately 30 seconds

13. ali ross skiing clinics

People are surprised when they find out that I still teach the recreational skiers who come to the Skiing Clinics myself. I think they expect that I coach only race trainees, for example, or other quite advanced skiers. This book has been devoted to showing you that anyone can learn to ski effectively. My aim in the Skiing Clinics is the same - to help you, the recreational skier, to understand what creates good skiing. When the Clinics first started as a system independent of national ski schools, the idea that recreational skiers should learn to carve their turns if they are to make real progress, was regarded as radical then and is still by no means universally accepted. Indeed it is still seen as almost heretical in some quarters. Some will say even to this day that, "Such techniques are only for racers". However new, modern ski design reflects the idea that carving should be the norm rather than the exception by producing skis with exaggerated side-cut, so that holiday skiers can learn to use the edges of their skis more easily and effectively, eliminating as much unnecessary skidding as possible. Our pupils have proven over the years in the Skiing Clinics that recreational skiers are able to use the same technique as the experts, at their own speeds and levels of skill and in doing so, discover that their skiing horizons have been widened immeasurably, sometimes surprising themselves.

Ali Ross Skiing Clinics offer a training programme based on the ideas and techniques examined in this book. At every level, from introductory through to advanced adventure weeks off-piste, clients are given consistency of information and feedback because I teach all courses myself. For this reason we have only two groups per week and at more advanced levels, just one.

A typical week might look something like this. There is a detailed introduction to the Clinic's programme on Sunday evening before dinner. This gives everyone the chance to meet the other members of the Clinic (if they don't already know one another, as many return as a group, having met on previous courses) and to ask any questions that they may have. The course proper begins on the Monday and finishes on the following Friday. On a two group course, I class pupils as far as possible with others of comparable ability. One group is taught in the morning and one in the afternoon, with a swop-over midweek and each receives at least two and a half hours concentrated tuition from me on the slopes every day. Built into the programme, therefore, is also time to practise what you have learned, either with the other members of your group or by yourself, as you prefer, in time for the next day's clinic. These practice times are a very important part of learning progress, if you are to get the most out of the programme.

The single group courses, who ski with me both mornings and afternoons, are primarily intended for those who are progressing through our system and who have therefore already completed the introductory course, but we are quite flexible if existing clients want to bring along friends who have not been with us before, but who could benefit from a course at this level.

Day One of the week's skiing will be videotaped and played back that evening to help you understand how you can improve your skills. You will be able to consolidate what you have learned and to ask any questions which you may have, in the early evening seminars, which are held on four evenings during the course. These usually last for a minimum of one hour.

As the Clinics are intended for intermediate and advanced skiers, there is a minimum standard. It is assumed that you have already mastered the basic skills and should be able to ski a red run competently. The Clinics are based in the French resort of Tignes, which has an enviable snow record and is therefore rated as one of the most snow-sure destinations in the Alps. Along with neighbouring Val d'Isere, it forms one of the largest ski areas in the world, both for on and off-piste skiing.

We also sometimes offer courses in North America.

For further information contact
Ski Solutions 0171 471 7777.

14. final thoughts

The theme running throughout this book is the importance of understanding what creates good skiing - the foundations of effective technique which will enable us to go where we want to in the mountains, within reason.

I spoke earlier about the origins of the Skiing Clinics, born to a large extent out of frustration with the conventional systems of teaching and of which I was part for a long while. Whilst my ideas about ski technique and teaching were evolving during my time as a ski school teacher, I could only offer a half-day or perhaps one day per week to the interested - and sometimes just the merely curious - private clients outside of the normal busy class arrangements of an Alpine ski school, for them to work upon the ideas which are now the basis of a week's course.

In the first season of the Skiing Clinics, a journalist once asked me, "Can all the others be wrong?", sceptical about the very notion that a recreational skier could ever improve using the basic design characteristics of the ski and the idea that the ski will turn you. Now, years later, to observe many of our original clients who had started out as scared intermediates, afraid of skiing a very average red run in Switzerland, skiing some of the more serious gullies in Tignes - or - the bird having flown the nest, as it were - regularly skiing the deep powder of the Canadian Rockies, is a reply which needs no further explanation and is more eloquent in itself than anything I could ever say. It is reassuring that modern ski technology has reinforced this response and therefore makes it easier to learn - or re-learn - how to ski, using the ski as it was meant to be used.

To put a book on any mountain sport into perspective, there are things which you can never learn from a book - the feedback, the setbacks, the encouragement, the high and low moments which are part of the challenge of learning generally. This is the reality of a week "on the hill", whatever weather prevails. I do however, hope that this book helps you on the way to achieve the goal of becoming a better skier.